The Budo Bum

Interview with Peter Boylan

The Aiki Dialogues - N. 15

The Budo Bum - Interview with Peter Boylan

Simone Chierchini

First edition

Publisher: The Ran Network
https://therannetwork.com

Front and Back Cover Photos © Peter Boylan

Cover and layout design by Simone Chierchini

ISBN: 9798369988299

Imprint: Independently published on Amazon KDP

Simone Chierchini

The Budo Bum

Interview with Peter Boylan

The Ran Network

乱
THE
RAN
NETWORK

Table of Contents

The Origins of the Budo Bum

"You named your personal blog *The Budo Bum* and the book that collects the best from it *Musings of a Budo Bum*. Why do you see yourself as a Budo Bum, besides the obvious reasons of being a humble and curious person?" [Simone Chierchini]

"*The Budo Bum* goes back to the 1990's and an email listserv for aikido known as *Aikido-L*. This was really the first place where *aikido* practitioners from all lineages engaged each other. There were already several active members on Aikido-L named Peter when I joined. To distinguish myself from the others, I started calling myself 'the budo bum'.

"In the United States, there are folks known as 'tennis bums' and 'golf bums'. These are people who are good enough to make a very modest living at tennis or golf but not good enough to compete in the big professional tournaments and such. They can travel from club to club working as a club pro teaching and playing.

"I see myself as being at that sort of level. I'm not a great martial artist, but I'm good enough that I have something to offer most people, while knowing that I can get a lot better.

"This ties into the American concept of the 'bum', which is a vagrant who wanders from place to place without settling down and without getting any sort of permanent job. They may do some begging as well as working odd jobs to pay their bills. In the 1990's I was living a rather carefree life. I graduated from university in 1990 and moved to Japan to learn Japanese for my master's degree and study *judo* while teaching English conversation to pay the bills.

"Another aspect of being a budo bum for me is that I'm open to trying whatever is available. I studied a number of different styles of aikido while working on my master's thesis, and I've been blessed to be able to taste many different *budo*. I've been able to try several different *koryu* schools over the years and expand my understanding. Bumming around the budo world has been fascinating and fun and I look forward to doing more of it. Being a budo bum for me is not just about bumming around doing the arts I know. It is about taking whatever opportunity presents itself for me to experience and learn about other budo forms.

"I've been quite lucky. My budo journey is closing in on 4 decades, and I still feel I am bumming around the budo world. I still have chances to train with *budoka* from many different styles and systems. I am thrilled every time I get to try a new art or train with someone new who is accomplished in their art."

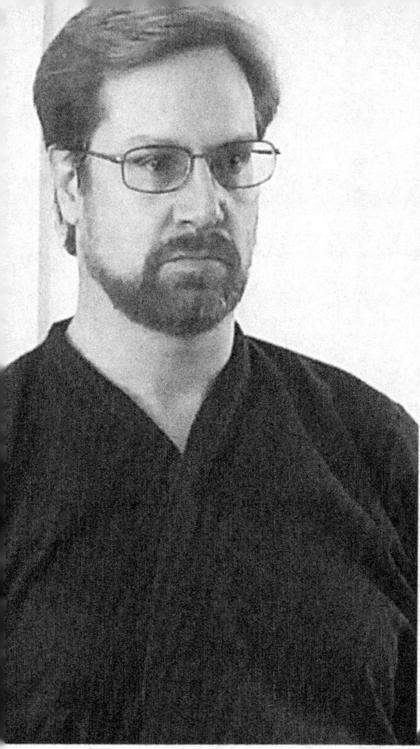

► *Yokaichi Koko Judo (1991)*

From Gendai to Koryu Budo

"What did you bring from your koryu studies in your *gendai* practice? And vice versa?" [Gabriele di Camillo]

"Good question. I hadn't really thought about this. My journey led from gendai into koryu budo, but it wasn't planned. Most of the big opportunities for me in budo were serendipitous. I started judo because I was looking for an active form of Daoist philosophy and I couldn't find *tai chi*. In the 1980's, pre-internet, there wasn't much information available, but what I could find suggested to me that judo had a similar philosophical bent. This should give you an idea of how little I knew starting out. I just got lucky that my university offered a judo class and had a very active judo club led by some very good teachers. I trained with the university club for 4 years.

"Then I graduated and moved to Japan. I lived in the relative countryside of Shiga Prefecture, about an hour outside of Kyoto. Like most Americans in Japan at that time, I was teaching English. I was lucky to make connections with the local high school club and a very good adult club. The judo *dojo* was the place I felt immediately at home in. The basic structure of the dojo was familiar, and because my university dojo emphasized learning the Japanese terminology I spoke fluent dojo judo. Those high school practices were intense. I could barely keep up when I first arrived. The adult group was a little less intense, but had a much broader social range, and I learned how to behave like an adult member in the dojo instead of as a student. I made all sorts of gaffes of course, but the dojo members were exceptionally generous and patient with me. I owe them a huge debt because they taught me not just advanced judo, but fundamental Japanese dojo behaviour and many, many lessons about Japanese culture and society.

"All of that training in judo dojos made it possible for me to fit into koryu training without too much difficulty. I knew the fundamentals of how to behave in the dojo and something about how to train. Training in a koryu is different though. The focus on developing skills through *kata* training rather than *randori* or competition took me quite a while to really understand and appreciate. I was coming from a judo background. Judo *keiko* usually started with *ukemi*, then 100 to 200 *uchikomi*, maybe some technique would be introduced and the last half or so would be randori. You could spend this time working with people on technique, but most people indulged in the chance to do 5-10 rounds of free sparring with friends and rivals. Randori can be very addictive. It's lots of fun to test yourself against others. Win or lose, I always had fun. I thought randori type practice was the goal of training.

"In the koryu that I do the focus is on kata training. From judo I knew how to behave and how to dedicate myself to practice. In koryu I learned the value of those kata that most *judoka* only do when they are preparing for a rank exam. Rather than being boring, over-scripted choreography, I discovered that kata could be lively, challenging training that is every bit as exhilarating as randori. Koryu taught me how doing something a hundred times could be interesting rather than boring. Approaching each time I did something as a unique chance to learn, I discovered that kata hold infinite

▶ *Peter Boylan, Jim Baker and Jun Akiyama*

variations and lessons.

"One of the biggest differences between koryu budo training and gendai budo training in Japan, in my limited experience, is the lack of formal structure in running the class. Gendai arts such as judo and *karate* and aikido and *kendo* have very structured training, with everyone practicing the same technique at the same time. The teacher leads the class and the students all focus on the same thing, whether that is practicing a technique or *kakari geiko* or any of the other things that go on in the dojo.

"The koryu dojos I practiced in, and continue to practice in when I can get to Japan, are not structured that way. The one that gave me the biggest shock was *iaido*. In the Kusatsu dojo, we practiced after the kendo keiko. The kendo keiko was very structured with everyone doing the same thing at the same time, including bowing in. The iaido keiko was completely different. If the gendai arts were structured to teach many people at one time, and to enforce common discipline, the iaido keiko expectation was that you would practice on your own initiative and that you were a mature person who didn't need group discipline. The iaido folks would wander in as the kendo keiko was going on, get changed and start warming up on their own. As the kendo class gradually cleared the floor, they were replaced by *iaidoka* one at a time. Each person would bow in to practice individually and start training on their own. There was no group bow at the beginning of practice. We each performed our bow to the *shomen* and our sword and started training. No one told you what to train. You picked something and worked at it. The senior teachers would train themselves, or walk around and give instruction individually. No two people would be working on the same kata. I would be practicing and would wander up to me and start fixing my form. After giving a few corrections they would wander away and leave me to work at integrating their corrections into my training. When we got close to 9:30, Sensei would call out

"*Yame*!" and we would stop what we were doing. Sensei would call out a couple of kata for us all to do together, always ending with the first kata everyone learns in the Kendo Federation, *Mae*. We would bow to our swords, bow to shomen, and then bow to each other in gratitude for the joy and privilege of practicing together.

"Coming from a gendai background, this took some adjustment. I wanted to be able to hide my ineptness at the back of the dojo where no one could see it while I tried to figure out how the seniors all moved with such grace and power. The way we were scattered around the dojo everyone could see what everyone else was doing. There was no hiding at the back of the class. There was also no guarantee that I would be told what to practice. I had to structure my own practice and the teachers would watch and decide what to teach me based on what they saw. I had to learn to rely on myself to choose the direction of my training each night.

"Gendai budo are designed for teaching large groups of people a common syllabus as one, and they are generally pretty good at it. Even if the teacher is not so good, the structure of the class generally prevents them from being too horrible. On the other hand, that very structure also prevents them from being too great as teachers. The students and teachers are both supported by that structure, and restrained from going outside of it.

"With koryu budo, a teacher is really on their own. The students will progress or not based as much on the teacher as on the effort the students put into it. If the teacher is phenomenal, training will have phenomenal results because there is nothing preventing the teacher from doing whatever they can think of to teach and support their students. On the other hand, if the teacher is lousy, the students may have to struggle to learn anything. Koryu live and die by the quality of those teaching them. One bad *soke* can kill a *ryuha*."

鹿島神武殿

Finding One's Place Through Training

"You have studied both gendai budo and *kobudo* for years. Broadly, what benefit do you believe you received from your gendai budo training and what benefit do you believe you received from kobudo? Were these benefits shaped by the particular arts themselves, by you or your approach at the time or both? How? [WT Gillespie]

"The judo dojo was the first place I ever felt truly comfortable. Just finding a place where I was welcome and comfortable was a huge benefit to me in many ways. Besides giving me a place where I felt comfortable and, surprisingly, safe, judo gave me quite a lot. I learned to have confidence in myself in a physical environment, something I'd never had before. I had always been the skinny, weak, pale, nerd who didn't fit in and didn't have a chance in a fight. Over the course of about 8 months, judo changed that dramatically, and by the end of my 2nd year of college judo, it may even have given me an inflated sense of my physical abilities. I never had anything come up that I wasn't able to handle, but that may be more luck than anything else. Judo made me effective in a one-on-one confrontation without weapons. I'm lucky I didn't walk myself into anything worse than that. The overconfidence probably came from the fact that we got a new class of beginning judo students every semester, and by the 4th semester, I was handling even the big new students without any trouble. I wasn't the best in the dojo, a lot of my friends were better than I was, but I was good enough to not be totally dominated by any of my friends, and able to control them often enough to not be discouraged.

"This idea that I was physically powerful was a brand new experience for me, having always been a skinny nerd. Now I was filling out, lifting some weights with dojo friends to improve my judo and getting good at being thrown around a room while throwing my partner around. People treated me as someone who shouldn't be messed with. I had to learn how to deal with that without becoming an arrogant jerk. I've seen enough people who did become jerks when they started to get some skill that I'm very glad my teachers and fellow students helped me avoid that trap.

"I learned how to behave in the dojo. For someone who had always been socially awkward at best, the structure of dojo relationships taught me how to interact with people from a range of backgrounds and different positions in the social hierarchy. Growing up I tended to think radical equality was the ideal way for people to get along. In the dojo I saw how people could get along with respect, even, perhaps especially, when they didn't see each other as being exactly equal. The Confucian structure of the dojo taught me a lot about social rituals that were very useful in the world outside of it, especially when I moved to Japan.

"The dojo is not a world of equality. It's a place where social rank is worn as a uniform by everyone. The colour and condition of your belt tells people a lot about your position in the dojo hierarchy. It is also a world built on mutual respect, at least in good dojos. The judo dojo taught me that people could be many different places on the social ladder and still treat each other with respect and dignity."

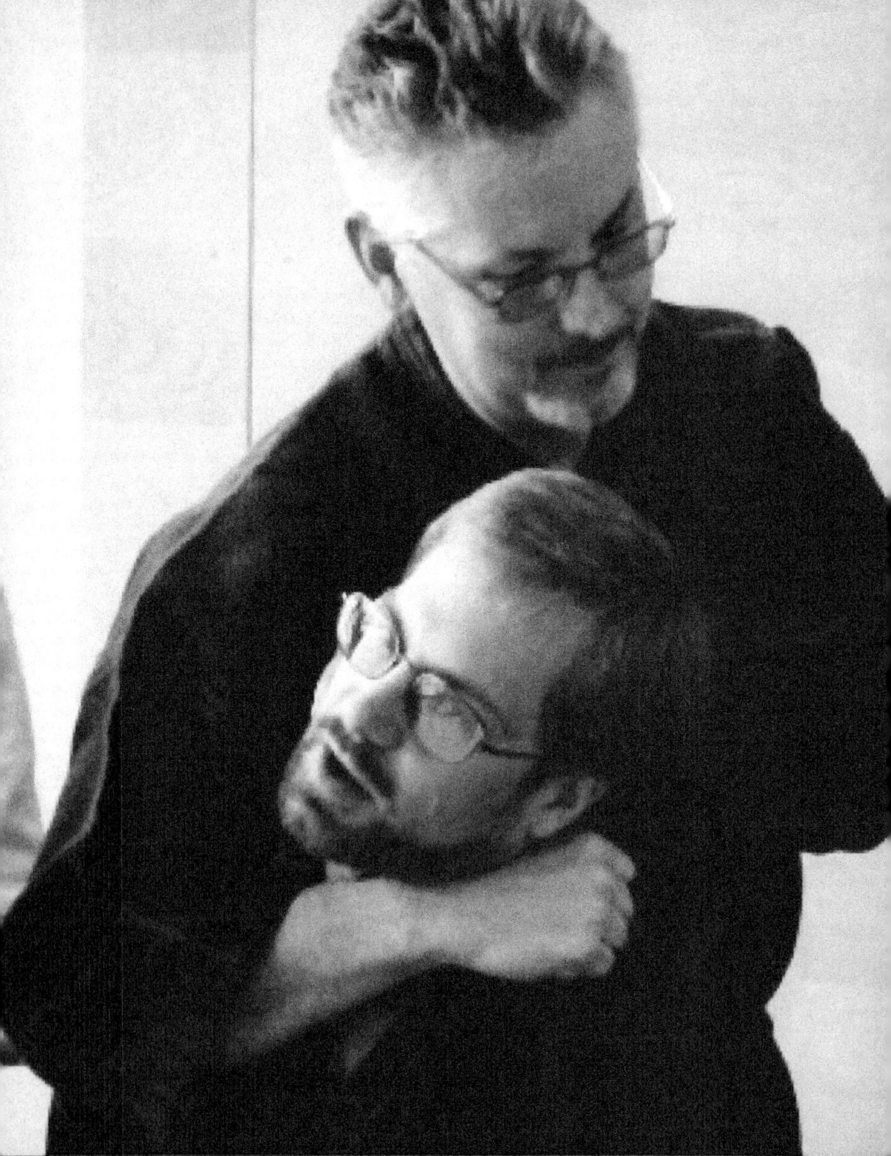

Budo and Physical Confrontation

"Narrowing the issue of benefits, could you articulate with some specificity whether (and if so how) the arts you've studied have contributed to your ability to defend yourself from a spontaneous physical confrontation, as opposed to match fighting." [WT Gillespie]

"This is something I haven't given much thought to in 20 years. Without question, the arts I study have contributed to my being able to handle physical confrontations. From being a pencil-necked geek who really didn't have much understanding of how to use his own body well, in just a handful of years judo taught me to trust my body and have confidence in my ability to handle physical confrontations. Koryu taught me discretion and gave me a broad understanding of spacing and timing. Nobody ever asks judoka 'Does judo really work?'. Judo randori is a test of your ability to use judo to control someone who is actively resisting being controlled. You get used to fighting people of all sizes and you learn to make your judo work on all of them. This builds a lot of confidence.

"I would say the biggest thing about dealing with a physical confrontation from judo is that getting hit is not the end of the fight. Pain hurts, but it's just pain. I learned to keep fighting even if something hurt. This was a powerful lesson for someone who had been bullied and fearful as a kid.

"I haven't had to use physical judo techniques often outside the dojo, in large part I think because judo practice made me confident that I could physically handle even someone significantly larger than me, and taught me that I didn't need to. I had enough confidence in myself that I didn't feel a need to rise to every challenge. Because I proved my ability every night in the dojo, I didn't feel any need to prove my ability outside the dojo. If someone was just being rude and looking for a fight, I could let them be an asshole without taking it personally and react in a way that deescalated the situation rather than letting rudeness rise to physical conflict.

"I also think the fact that I don't follow the normal 'script' for a fight helps. My voice doesn't get loud. I don't get angry or upset. After all of the people who have thrown me around the dojo, choked me or arm-barred me, I don't have any ego involved in a street fight. I'm calm and quiet no matter how loud and how close to my face someone gets. People don't seem to want to get in a fight with a person who isn't angry or upset, but who remains calm and cool regardless of what is said to them or how much posturing someone does.

"When I was living in Japan, I worked teaching English in a pretty rough school at one point. This school had a small gang of kids who ignored all the rules, did whatever they felt like doing and who were not accustomed to anyone telling them they couldn't do what they wanted to. I didn't make friends with them by repeatedly preventing them from disrupting class or causing other problems around the school. At one point I came across one of them outside the building during class time holding an ice pick. Weapons being banned in school, I told him to give it to me. Instead, he swung it at me. He swung it a few times and as it went past, I reached for an arm bar. I didn't get the grip I was looking for, but the force of my hand smacking into the back of the student's

EXIT

wrist and hand knocked his hand open and he dropped the ice pick. He dove after the ice pick, and as he was grabbing it on the ground, I stepped on his hand. That was the end of that.

"I learned a huge amount from this experience. When the student started waving that ice pick at me, it couldn't have been more than about 10 cm long, but my brain reacted like he had something the length of a sword. It took a few swings before I started to understand the real length and reach of the weapon. All of my judo up to this time had been based around competitive Olympic style judo training. I hadn't done much with any of the judo kata, and nothing with any of the kata that deal with strikes and weapons attacks. I realized I had no idea of how to deal with weapons attacks, and my plan for dealing with strikes revolved around closing inside an opponent's range and grappling. This was before the Gracies invented the UFC and gave birth to MMA, and before the internet, so these ideas weren't all over the place yet.

"This experience prompted me to start looking at the kata of Kodokan Judo with an eye to actually learning something rather than just learning enough to pass my next rank test. There are a couple of judo kata that teach quite a bit about dealing with strikes and basic weapons attacks, and I made a point to learn something about them.

"A couple of years after this, I started doing *Muso Jikiden Eishin Ryu iai* and *Shinto Muso Ryu jo*. One of the first things I learned from doing the paired kata exercises in these koryu was that I had no clue about the real *maai* of weapons or what they could do. The judo kata I was practicing taught counters to weapon attacks. From koryu though, I learned that if the person wielding the weapon is not skilled with it, you won't learn much about dealing with the weapon from the kata practice. Weapons spacing and timing is different from unarmed spacing and timing. This seems obvious, but I didn't understand and appreciate the degree of difference until I started training with weapons experts.

"The range at which a swordsman can impale you before you can react is a lot further than you think. A skilled practitioner with a weapon can cover more distance in less time than I ever imagined before weapons training. The ability of my teachers to put a sword in an opening that I didn't even realize was there made me understand that my judo would be useless against someone with even modest weapons training. It took many years of weapons training before I felt that I had any chance going unarmed against a skilled weapons handler. Even after nearly 30 years of weapons training, I would put my chances of doing anything successful against a skilled weapons handler at poor. Weapons are just too fast, and they take advantage of the additional attacking range too well.

"At this point I would say that the best things I have for dealing with physical confrontation after all these years of gendai and koryu budo training are an appreciation for how risky any sort of fight is, and the ability to breathe. Breathing is fundamental, but under any sort of stress we tend to forget to breathe, and even when we don't forget, we usually do it badly. At this point in my training good breathing is something that I don't think about. It happens automatically most of the time, and it has become my default reaction to stress. In a confrontation I can manage my breathing, and through that, maintain my calm and my composure."

► *Koboto Santaro, a Japanese military commander, by Felice Beato, ca. 1868*

Classical Kata Is a Road Map for Your Training

"The level of mastery in the classical Japanese arts is achieved by following a definite and progressive structure of study. Can a beginner approaching a Koryu today expect that by following its path with full commitment and persistence he will be able to attain a level of awareness and ability similar to that of the specialists of that Koryu in the past?" [Simone Chierchini]

"Specialists of which period? The late Muromachi era? The early Tokugawa era? The late Tokugawa era? Real specialists were always relatively rare. Most people have more important things to do that endlessly practice how to hurt, maim and kill each other.

"It's difficult to imagine anyone having the time and resources to devote half a day, 6 days a week, to martial arts training for years on end. The Yoshinkan Kenshusei course is one of the few examples where that sort of training is still seen, and even that is a one year course. I was lucky enough during university that I could train judo at least 4 days a week for 2-4 hours at a time. The level being asked about though is more akin to being an Olympic athlete than what most of us do. There are judo and kendo practitioners who are privileged to train that way and work as professional police instructors in Japan. Even for people who won't be professionals, there is the International Budo University in Chiba Prefecture., where you can study budo intensively for 4 years.

"Most of us don't have the time to train like that, but neither did most people in the Muromachi and Tokugawa eras. They had more important things to do, such as earn enough to feed and care for their families. What they did have was a very different lifestyle. They walked everywhere. They regularly carried heavy loads and worked hard every day, whether it was working in a field or maintaining a household or running a business. They worked their bodies in ways very few people in industrialized countries do. Weight training and cardio will give you strength and stamina, but not the sort that someone who grows up working in fields and other labor will have. The body just develops differently when you sit in a chair studying most of the time. I think this does make a difference in what sort of results we can achieve.

"I also know that while we have not hardened our bodies by plenty of manual labor from an early age, we have also not stressed them from living through long periods of time with insufficient calories and nutrition. This makes a difference as well. Food insecurity and outright famine were common throughout the history of Japan. People were small in stature because of insufficient nutrition. This undoubtedly prevented even the best of practitioners from reaching their full potential.

"The closest I can come to the old masters are a few of the people I have trained with. Men who started training in martial arts in the 1930s when most agriculture in Japan was still hard labor. Omori Masao Sensei was a great kendo and iaido teacher. He did powerful iaido into his 90s. My teacher, Kiyama Hiroshi Sensei, was powerful into his 90's as well. Are they better than the masters of the Tokugawa era? I wasn't there, so I can't say. I do know they trained hard and

► Omori Masao

pushed themselves to become accomplished budoka.

"If we talk about someone training hard in koryu and becoming as accomplished as the specialists of another era, I will say that I think that the pedagogy left to us in the form of the classical kata do offer a road map for getting the most of your training, and forging the finest martial artist the raw material you bring with you can become. The training methods work. If they didn't they would have been driven into extinction hundreds of years ago by something better. The fact that koryu systems survived hundreds of years when challengers were plentiful is proof that the koryu systems for training students consistently create well trained students.

"Whatever level students of the arts achieved in the past is not really relevant to practicing today though. Whether we can't achieve the same levels because our modern life has made our bodies too soft, or we can easily surpass the physical achievements of old because we have better nutrition and health care is not, I think, all that important. The various budo provide paths for development and the real question is how far do we go with the bodies and minds we have. In every era students come to the dojo with a variety of skills, talents, physical gifts and handicaps. That has always been true. Something else that has always been true is that it is up to the student to do as much as they can with what they have. I have students whose physical gifts are quite limited, but they put in effort and they make progress. Will they become great masters of budo? No. Do I think they will benefit from the training and that the dojo benefits from including them in our training? Yes. It was never the case that most people would rise to the highest levels of the arts.

"The majority of students never reach menkyo kaiden or similar license. They don't train with that as their goal. They train to learn and develop themselves as much as they can through training in their ryuha. I think that's all anyone in any era can do. We train, and through training we develop our minds and bodies in the principles of our arts. Some will always go further than others. While I think it should always be a goal of a teacher to develop students who are better than they are, it's not always possible. Sometimes a teacher can't find a student who exceeds them. That's okay. Within koryu, the kata pedagogy will allow following generations to climb as high as they are able. Gendai budo aren't so new that they have histories that go up and down, but the ones that will survive in the long term are the ones that have a solid method for training new students in their principles. The ones that don't will fade and disappear.

"Looking back at the original question, I would add that a beginner entering a koryu should not expect that they can reach the highest levels of the art. Most of us will never get there. Even moderate skill in a koryu is a big thing and requires a lot of effort. The most that a student should expect is to learn a lot. Whether or not they reach the highest echelon of the art shouldn't be a concern. It's the journey. There is no destination.. Any time you spend thinking about a destination is time taken away from training in the now. That's the important thing. Training now."

文武不岐

Budo Training Is not for Everyone

"In a recent article, you stated the following: 'I have arrived at the position that budo training is not for everyone. The teachings of classical budo ryuha are effective, and students should have the maturity and discretion to know when to use them, and when not to. I have known many people who are middle-aged or older, but have the maturity of an adolescent. As a teacher of a classical ryuha, it is my responsibility not to put the ryu's treasures in the hands of anyone who will misuse or abuse them. We often hear about what people deserve. There is no mandate that anyone deserves to learn a koryu bugei ryuha. Even in the 21st century these arts are precious and should be treated as such'. Now, I would like to ask you how you carry out this responsibility to select or filter." [John Bailey]

"How do I manage quality control in my own dojo is a very good question and one I've given a lot of thought to. I don't think there is a simple answer. I start by talking with anyone who wants to start training with me. People's attitudes are important. Why do they want to train? What do they think they will get out of training? There is no correct answer to these questions, but what people say in response to them tells me a lot about their motivations. I've had people interview with me whom I did not want to come back, and so far I've been lucky. The ones my gut didn't like also didn't like me enough to come back, so I didn't have to tell them to go away. I don't know if they picked up my disapproval or not, but it has worked out that way so far..

"One thing that I think helps is that koryu bugei are pretty obscure, even in the Japanese martial arts community. Most Japanese can't name any koryu beyond perhaps Niten Ichi Ryu and Yagyu Shinkage Ryu. The only reason they might know those names is because there have been famous books and television shows about Miyamoto Musashi and various members of the Yagyu clan. People with attitudes I don't want in my dojo don't seem to be attracted to koryu bugei. They aren't famous and they aren't flashy. If you're not interested in the journey of training, they are also boring. We spend a lot of time on kihon, and even when we're not focusing on kihon, we talk about the fundamentals a lot.

"I watch the people in my dojo. How do they behave towards each other? How do they behave in the dojo? Do they show respect for other people? Do they show respect for the art? Little things are important. How do they treat their weapons? Does their reiho feel sincere or are they just going through the motions because I say they have to.

"I've had far more problems with people in judo than I have in koryu. Judo is as open as a martial art can be, and it has penetrated popular culture enough that it attracts people with all sorts of attitudes. I have been involved in escorting people out of the dojo for completely unacceptable behavior. Those are easy decisions. The tough ones are the men (it always seems to be men) who are just a little bit bad. The ones who don't pay attention when a teacher is talking to the group, or who are a little careless with their training partners. These are the difficult calls to make.

"How much leeway do I give someone to misbehave while they are learning to be good members of the dojo? How many times do I have to explain to someone that their

► *Yagyu Family Kamon*
©Takeda-art

behavior is disrespectful towards the teachers, or their fellow students, or to judo itself? I try to be patient to a fault with these people. I want to give them every opportunity to learn. I will talk with them time and again and patiently give them instruction in what respectful behavior is and what it indicates to people. When they convince me that they have no interest in learning, and no intention of changing, that's when we start having talks about how inappropriate behavior

► *Jigoro Kano*

is not welcome in the dojo. I also start suggesting arts that might be more appropriate for them, if I can think of any. So far everyone has gotten the point and found someone else to practice with.

"I have a lot less patience with the people who don't have complete respect for the health and safety of their training partners. I keep reading that Kano Jigoro Shihan took all the dangerous techniques out of judo. I've got news for folks, what's left in judo is plenty dangerous, especially if you're not paying any attention to what you are doing to your training partners. Throws that put uke neatly on the ground so uke can take good ukemi become extremely dangerous when you're not worried about getting your partner to the ground safely. I've been injured by people who didn't care about my health and safety, and I don't want folks like that in my dojo. Accidents do happen, especially in randori, but if I see someone repeatedly attempt risky, dangerous techniques or insist on pushing everything to extremes, someone who won't modulate the power in their techniques to be appropriate for the person they are training with and just throw everyone with full power and full speed every time, I start a conversation with that person. It's my duty as a teacher to challenge my students and teach them to the best of my ability. It's also my responsibility to make sure they go home healthy after every practice. When I see a dangerous pattern of behavior I'll have a few talks with the person. If they won't listen and change, then I'll suspend their training privileges for a few weeks. If that doesn't work, then it becomes a couple of months. I've never seen anyone insist on coming back after a longer suspension. They usually find somewhere else to play their games."

Budo Happens All the Time

"The mechanics, how-to, metrics of this are something I spend much time considering. Principles don't change. That's the nature of principles. They are fundamental ways of understanding the world and how it operates. In budo, sometimes principles are expressed and learned through physical practice. Principles, by their nature, are universal. If they can't be applied universally, they aren't principles. I very much agree with this understanding. These are things I say in both budo and in the other fields in which I work. How they are applied and expressed changes all the time however. Not because the principles change at all, but because the environment in which they are being applied changes. Do they stop doing judo because they take off their dogi and fight in competitions that aren't using IJF rules? If you're applying judo principles it's still judo, regardless of what you're wearing or what you're doing. Budo practices are paths to follow, not fossils. You have to adapt to the terrain. My sensei used to say 'If it works, it's Aikido' - so you can imagine how much I agree with his statement. I'm interested in your thoughts about this adaptive process." [John Bailey]

"People get hung upon the techniques of an art. As the

saying goes, 'they miss the forest for the trees'. Arts are not made up of techniques. They are made up of principles, and techniques are how we learn the principles. To use an old Daoist analogy, they are the finger pointing at the moon. We're supposed to follow where the finger is pointing and see that, not the finger. If we get hung up on the finger, we will never see the moon. The relationship between the principles that are the heart of the art and the techniques that we practice is the same as the moon and the pointing finger. Once you master the principles, the techniques disappear. I've been doing budo for over 35 years now (which seems like a very short career to me. My iai teacher, Kiyama Hiroshi, started jujutsu at the age of five. He just passed away at 97, and he was teaching me things until the end. I figure I have a long way to go.) Budo happens all the time for me. It's integral to the person I am, physically and mentally. This is because budo is the principles, not any particular set of techniques. Judo and iaido and jodo all inform the way I move. Walking is budo. Breathing is budo. The techniques we practice in the dojo are not budo. They are tools for learning budo. If you are studying aikido, your goal is not to master a particular set of techniques. Your goal is to master the principles of aikido so that you can express those principles anywhere, under any circumstances. I study Kodokan Judo, among other things. The wonderful thing about judo randori is that you end up in all sorts of situations that aren't covered in the standard techniques. A student is starting to absorb and express the principles of judo when they come off the mat having just thrown someone beautifully, and they have no idea what throw they did. I have been congratulated for a great throw, and I had to ask "What did I do?" The action was so quick I didn't think about it, I just did it, and what I did may not even be a named judo "technique" but it was judo because I was expressing the principles of judo in some way. The deeper the principles permeate your bones, the more often

► *Hiroshi Kiyama and Peter Boylan*

► Yoshiteru Otani

things like this happen, on and off the mat. There are a finite number of techniques in judo and aikido, but only a few principles that can be expressed in an infinite number of ways. I've seen students "invent" techniques when they realized how to apply a principle. I once choked someone out with my chin in randori. We were rolling around on the ground, and I suddenly realized that if I stuck my chin just *there*, I could finish a strangle. I did, and it worked. There are some fundamental principles that have to be applied for judo strangles. At that moment I understood the principles deeply enough to spontaneously see a way of strangling someone with one hand and my chin. The opportunity appeared as we were rolling around seeking control.

"Kano Jigoro and Ueshiba Morihei both wrote about the universal nature of the arts they founded. They weren't talking about ways of fighting. I'm sure there is no technique in judo or aikido that the grappling masters of ancient Egypt didn't know or would have been surprised by. What is unique about them is that they are supposed to be teaching us something more than just techniques for breaking wrists and arms or throwing people at the ground. You're supposed to imbibe the principles and then express them naturally throughout your life outside the dojo. We study the techniques to learn the principles. Ueshiba Morihei famously said that "there are no techniques in Aikido". I would agree with that, and I would say that there are no techniques in judo or Shinto Muso Ryu or Shinto Hatakage Ryu. In studying any budo we start out by studying techniques, but the techniques are not the art. The principles are the art.

"When you understand the principles you can forget the techniques" is something that Yoshiteru Otani Sensei (teacher of my friend Deborah Klens-Bigman) said. When I first heard it, it made little sense to me. Now the meaning seems obvious. I've stopped looking at the finger and now I see the moon. I'm not sure it's possible to fully express the principles of any budo in words alone. The principles are more fundamental than words. We have to learn them through living them. The first step to living them is modeling them. That's what techniques and kata are for, modeling the principles. Judo has 65 throws in the classical curriculum. Those just begin to express the way the principles of judo can be applied. First you practice techniques. Then you try to apply the techniques in randori. Then you begin to sense the principles and you fight to express them through the techniques that you study. Eventually you gain enough mastery to successfully apply the principles in randori through the techniques you're practicing. It's only when you can apply the principles spontaneously without doing one of the techniques you practice that I think you are approaching real understanding of them.

"The principles of budo are expressed in 4 dimensions. You can do judo without ever touching someone. This can be something where you convince people to flow around you in a crowd, or you can flow around them. Either way you're employing judo. You can apply kuzushi physically by the way you move. You can do the same thing socially through what you say or how you direct a conversation. These principles are profound and fundamental. I think they are so profound that language is not adequate for expressing them. They have to be lived to be understood. Techniques and kata provide a way for us to experience the principles and learn to apply them, and if we are diligent, to express them spontaneously.

"I used to say that we learn to adapt the principles to the situation. I'm not sure if this is the right way to think about it. The principles are always there. They are part of the fabric of existence. I think, like the time I created a strangle with my chin, we learn to recognize them in the world around us. The best aikido and judo techniques are the ones where uke gets up off the floor and says "What happened?

▶ *Paolo N. Corallin*

► *Morihei Ueshiba*

I didn't feel anything." Tori hasn't adapted the principles to the situation. Tori understood how the principles could be expressed in the moment and guided things so the principles could express themselves. Like Cook Ding guiding his knife so smoothly through the ox that he never needs to sharpen it, we learn to move with and express the principles of our budo.

"It's easy to talk about some of the principles of Kodokan Judo because Kano Jigoro gave some of them clear names. Kuzushi. Jita Kyoei. Seiryoku Zen'yo. But putting the principles into words often limits our understanding of them rather than deepening it. "Kuzushi" is often (mis) translated as "off-balancing". Once people start thinking of it as off-balancing, they become trapped in a much smaller concept than kuzushi 崩し. Off-balancing is one way of expressing kuzushi, but it's not the only one. The thing that impressed me when I first encountered good aikido was the excellent kuzushi. People talk about this mysterious "aiki" but when I grab hold of someone who has really good "aiki" I sense their application of kuzushi on me. They are, as my friend Michael Hacker so eloquently puts it, undermining my foundation. This is a much deeper meaning than just "off-balancing". I don't think "undermining the foundation" completely encapsulates all that is "kuzushi" but it comes far closer than any other verbal definition I've seen. The only way to truly understand kuzushi is to experience it and practice it. Words can only capture a portion of what's happening when kuzushi is applied.

"That's why we have to practice kata (yes, I know Ueshiba said there are no kata in Aikido, but standard Aikido practice is exactly kata). Those deeper meanings can't be grasped from a book or a lecture (I do get the irony of saying this in a book about budo). Through kata practice we learn to sense the principles and then to apply them. At first we can only apply them within the framework of the kata of practice. Slowly our understanding broadens and deepens so we can see the expression of the principles everywhere.

"Budo, if it's done right, should influence every aspect of our lives. It should inform the physical; how we walk, how we breathe, how we hold our bodies when we're standing still or sitting down. It should inform the mental; how we remain calm even under emotional attacks, that we aren't threatened by violent threats, that we approach everything with a mind that is still and focused and undisturbed by extraneous activities.

"If you're truly doing budo, you're applying it all the time, to everything you do outside the dojo. You don't do budo in the dojo. You practice it in the dojo. Doing budo happens after you bow out and leave the floor. That's when you start applying budo principles. A goal of any budo training is to be able to apply it all the time you're NOT in the dojo. What we do in the dojo is practice so that when we leave we can do budo. That requires us to adapt the principles of our art to whatever situation we find ourselves in. Budo principles are always there, ready to be applied, if we understand them well enough."

Adapting Budo

"I see some people creating differences for the sake of "new" - perhaps to help prevent becoming bored – or as another sensei used to say "disguising repetition from the mind". I see other people already operating in an environment (e.g. police) – who are introduced later to budo principles – and then adapting or asking instructors to help them adapt – into that specific set of needs. I'd like to ask you about what, in your view, is a sound basis for finding or creating adaptation – and what, if anything, is not a sound basis for altering how things are done? When, how, why do we adapt our art? When, and why, do we choose to hold instead to tradition?" [John Bailey]

"I have no problem with adapting our arts. If they can't be adapted to new conditions and situations, they aren't worth much. The techniques and kata of an art are the starting point, not the end point. Budo has to be flexible and adaptable. A martial art that isn't flexible enough to adapt to new conditions isn't worth much. Classical ryuha have survived hundreds of years, through changes in culture and technology unimaginable when they were founded, and yet many people still find great value in them.

"The classical budo forms, the koryu, are not meant to be unchanging fossils whose ideas and practice are carved in stone. Instead they are known as "ryu" 流. The base meaning of the character is "flow, stream, current". The metaphor is one of flowing water, which takes the shape of whatever vessel it encounters yet can wear away mountains. A stream is not static and unchanging. If you follow the Mississippi River to its source, you find that it starts as a very small stream. As it travels across the land it gathers other streams and rivers into itself, constantly changing as its waters increase and the landscape changes.

"Budo ryuha are similar. Take for example Shinto Muso Ryu. It started as just a few kata for jo versus sword, and a set of sword versus sword kata. Over the centuries more and more kata for the jo were added, and other weapons absorbed into the curriculum until we have the art as it is practiced today, encompassing jo, tachi, kodachi, kusarigama, jutte, hojojutsu and tanjo. It has grown and branched many, many times over the last 100 years since it left Fukuoka. There are some lines that have recently added iai kata to their practice to improve their sword work. With the selection of weapons taught, Shinto Muso Ryu manages to teach principles of the stick that can be applied to any length stick a human can readily wield. Over the centuries, as various Shinto Muso Ryu teachers saw a need for adaptation or for expanding practitioners' understanding, they created new kata and absorbed other arts to fill any holes they perceived in the curriculum. Kusarigama is a wildly different weapon from the sticks that make up the majority of Shinto Muso Ryu, and it teaches students about handling and dealing with an entirely different class of weapons. Chain and rope weapons behave very differently from sticks and need their own training.

"All koryu arts have changed and adapted over the centuries. The ones that can't adapt their principles to new circumstances will become fossilized museum pieces and die. Adaptation may be creating new kata for the existing weapons (even if those weapons are empty hands) or it

► *Muso Gonnosuke Katsuyoshi, Shinto Muso Ryu originator*

► *Vintage Shinto Muso Ryu jodo*

could mean applying the ryuha's principles to a new weapon. This is what happened in the 19th century when Uchida Ryogoro moved to Tokyo and saw English walking sticks become fashionable. He took the principles of the jo and applied them to the much shorter walking sticks that were suddenly all over Tokyo. The resulting kata were thought worthwhile to preserve in the curriculum of Shinto Muso Ryu. There are techniques for arrest and control that are taught in some lines as kuden, or "oral tradition". They aren't included in any scrolls and they don't have a special name, but they exist. I can easily see future menkyo kaiden adding other weapons and even jujutsu techniques to the curriculum if they see a need for them. This kind of adaptation can be found in the history of many koryu, and it will continue to happen. Koryu are "old traditions", not fossils.

"The same should be true of gendai arts, but I'm afraid the politics of trying to make changes to adapt the principles of judo or aikido or karate to something not already in their curriculums would tear apart the committees that govern them. This leads to people taking what they have learned and creating a new system because the politics of the older art doesn't leave any room for adaptation. This doesn't mean that adaptation isn't happening, it means that it is happening in an unsanctioned way.

"To return to an earlier theme, the techniques and kata are the finger pointing at the moon, the principles are the moon. Whatever the art, taking the principles and applying them to new situations is something that should happen. Police officers come into judo and aikido dojos all the time to learn. They learn the principles of the art and then they work out how to apply those principles in their jobs. They are still doing judo or aikido when they do this at work, they just aren't wearing the funny pajamas and limiting themselves to the techniques that are tested when you want to advance in rank. In one way I would say that the people adapting the principles so they can be applied in everyday life are the ones truly doing the art. The folks who go to the dojo, practice the techniques or kata, then go home and do nothing with what they have learned aren't doing budo. They're just going through the motions. You're not really doing budo until you're applying it outside the dojo.

"I do not think the proliferation of modern styles is a good trend, and the value of most of these new styles is apparent in their lifespan. The vast majority of "new" martial arts don't last very long. They appear in someone's marketing, and disappear when their creator stops teaching them. They don't have enough depth or solid enough foundations to survive. This has been true of martial arts for as long as I have seen records. The Bugei Ryuha Daijiten is an encyclopedia of all the ryuha the authors could find records of in Japan. It's a thick book, with thousands of ryuha listed. The vast majority of them only lasted a few generations. Very few of them had the depth and principles and good luck to survive into the 21st century.

"I don't think it's a case of "holding on to tradition". With good budo, the fundamentals and an effective way of teaching them have long been known. With each student we have to start by teaching them the fundamentals. They can't start adapting and applying the principles outside the dojo until they master them inside the dojo. We hold onto the foundations of our arts because those provide the base upon which we build our skills to the point that we can adapt and apply them in new scenarios that the founders of the art may never have envisioned.

"Changes for the sake of change, or worse, changes for the sake of popularity, are never good ideas. I look at what has been done to judo in the last 30 years for the sake of making it more telegenic so that the Olympic Committee won't drop it as an Olympic sport and become very angry. Techniques have been removed not because too many

people were being injured or they had too much risk of causing fatal injuries when done properly. No, techniques have been banned from competition because they don't promote big, telegenic throws, and they are too similar to wrestling techniques. Judo has to stand out and be popular with audiences to stay in the Olympics. I think it's a lousy tradeoff. Even worse is what has happened to Tae Kwon Do in the Olympics. I can't watch it. Budo are not spectator sports. They are martial ways whose principles have to be respected or they become nothing more than entertainment.

"Budo are very conservative. As a rule they are skeptical of change. In the case of koryu, they have been effective for hundreds of years. If it has worked for that long, there would have to be a very strong reason to change the way things are done. In general, if it is determined that there is something a ryuha needs that is not currently found in that ryuha, instead of changing what is there, something will be added to the ryuha."

► *Keiko Fukuda*

Balancing Different Levels of Practice

"The proportion of waza practice versus randori practice versus kata practice is something judoka never stop arguing about, and every judo dojo has a different answer to what the proportions should be. My own writing about this is "levels of contrivance" - that is my lens. I would like to hear about your lens – your ideas about the balancing of these various levels of practice – and most importantly about the underlying principles on which you base those ideas." [John Bailey]

"When it comes to training, I'm fairly old school. I think the emphasis should be on fundamentals training and kata, with randori type practice thrown in for fun. Some of this comes not from my experience with budo, but from learning and playing musical instruments. You can't train for combative situations by repeatedly going out and getting into fights. Well, you could try, but I think most people who attempt this path will end up being badly beaten many times before they start to learn anything from the experience.

"All of our training is contrivance to avoid that path.

"In music, you spend a huge chunk of your time just doing fundamental exercises. For advanced musicians this can be as much as 20% of their practice time. This is the time spent doing warm-ups, basic scales, arpeggios and fingering exercises. Then there are etudes which train more difficult movements and techniques. It's only after doing all of these fundamental practices that musicians move on to studying and practicing musical pieces, and that practice is rarely playing the piece from beginning to end without stopping. More often it is taking small portions of the piece and working on them until these little bits are good before maybe playing the piece beginning to end. Practice is grounded in the fundamentals, and it is going beyond mastering the fundamentals until you do them as readily as you breathe and walk. When the fundamentals reach this level, picking up a new piece of music and sight reading it (playing the music when you look at it the first time) is no problem. In the jazz world there used to be "fake books" which just had the melody and the chord structures. A group of competent musicians could flip to a song they'd never played before and make it sound good as a group with just the melody and the chords because they had everything else they needed from their fundamentals practice. I doubt fake books are a thing anymore. Now everyone probably just carries an iPad for reference.

"Budo practice should be similar; lots of basic exercises. This starts with things like weight training and stretching. These have to be considered part of your budo practice. They are just like a musician playing scales and other basic activities. If the body isn't kept in good condition nothing else can be improved. That old iai line that "everything you need to know about iaido is in the first kata" is true for most things in budo.

"That first kata includes proper posture and body integration, how to move, how to breathe, and how to handle the weapon. I sometimes think that the main reason for having more than just the one kata is to prevent new students from getting too bored until they realize everything they need to learn is in the first kata.

"For another example, look at how Olympic judoka train.

► *Yoshio Sugino, Tenshin Shoden Katori Shinto Ryu*

► *Jigoro Kano and Kenzo Mifune*

They spend a huge amount of their time on stretching, strength training, and movement drills before they even start with technique practice. They drill techniques endlessly. Then they do kata practice. No, not the classical kata of Kodokan Judo, but kata nevertheless. They practice prearranged attack and defense forms for entering and executing techniques. That's all kata is. They might have their partner set up in a particular stance, and they'll practice the movements for creating an opening and executing a throw against that stance. That's a kata, it's just not a formal, named kata of the Kodokan.

"Kata aren't only the formal, named movements of a ryuha. Those are just the ones that get preserved and passed down from generation to generation. There are plenty of spontaneously developed kata for drilling particular techniques or movements. This fundamental practice is where we really learn budo. The foundation of budo practice is repetition of movement sequences until those happen without conscious thought. With physical conflict, there isn't time for conscious competence. Your competence has to be unconscious. Only then can you really start playing with it.

"You can experiment and play with your budo anywhere along the line. I often have students ask me 'what if' questions. Most often the answer to these questions is 'That's covered in a different kata you haven't learned yet', but sometimes the answer is 'Try it and let's see what we get'. Doing a more than 400 year old art like Shinto Muso Ryu, every time we've played with something like this, we've discovered compelling reasons why the kata is done in a certain way. When we try to change things we discover that the kata holds a better way of dealing with that specific situation than anything we can come up with. It's always enlightening.

"Even within kata, experimenting happens. Shinto Muso Ryu has more than 60 kata, but only 12 fundamental techniques. It's not surprising then that many kata share moments where shijo finds themselves in a position that is the same as in previously learned kata. I hesitate to count the number of times we step into hiki ototshi no kamae or gyaku hiki otoshi no kamae. In each kata we take a different path forward. Sometimes we forget which kata we are doing and mix the path forward from another kata. You have to hope that your partner at that moment has the awareness and experience to simply respond to what you are doing rather than what the kata says comes next. This happens a lot when people are learning a new kata, particularly Ran Ai.

"To really learn and get the principles of any art into your bones you must experiment and play with it. Some arts, such as judo and karate do this with open competitions. Most aikido styles include unstructured practice called randori, which is very different from judo randori, but which also provides a way for people to practice applying the fundamental principles of aikido in a free flowing situation. Experimentation and play are important, but they can't happen effectively until you have the basic drilled into your bones. I think fundamentals practice should be 10-20% of any training session, kata should be 70-80%, while experimentation and play should not be more than 10%.

"As important as experimentation and play are, they are useless if the foundations aren't there. Jazz musicians drill scales and chord progressions endlessly, so that when the time comes to perform they can make the changes and adapt to the music without having to give what they are doing conscious thought. Even more so for improvisation. If you have to think about it, you're not ready for it. You won't be able to keep up with the music if you're thinking about what to do next.

"The same problem exists in randori and sparring situations in budo. If you have to think about it, you're too late. You've already been hit or thrown or submitted.In my opinion, people start randori and sparring much too early,

► *The author with Deborah Klens-Bigman*

and are much too attached to the goal of "winning". This gets in the way of really learning the art, and is a big reason so many of us develop bad habits. Randori and sparring are fun, and everyone likes the validation that winning gives. Most of us start out doing randori and sparring long before our fundamentals are solid, and this leads to bad habits. We end up relying on muscle instead of good technique. We develop bad technical habits because in the isolated world of randori and competition they help us "win". Unfortunately, what helps us to victory over other green belts generally isn't clean technique with strong, upright posture. It's strength and gumption that get us through matches at that stage, and so we learn to rely on our physical strength and bad habits like holding people out with stiff arms or being so defensive it's difficult to respond to openings when they appear."

► *Ellis Amdur, Araki Ryu*

Training Without Martial Core

"Taking into account your wide experience in the field, do you think that Budo could effectively find a new niche in the relationship arts without completely losing its martial side? More specifically, can Budo be expected to be useful as a method of conflict resolution once it has lost its martial attributes? As time goes by, Budo's technical and martial core, which have always been its essence and from which all its utilitarian/social extra-martial functions have been derived until now, has declined. How effective can a weak and watered down Budo be at a relational level?" [Simone Chierchini]

"I would disagree with the fundamental premise that "Budo's technical and martial core, …has declined." The Shinto Muso Ryu that I practice, the Katori Shinto Ryu that I see demonstrated at Meiji Jingu, the Araki Ryu that Ellis Amdur teaches, the Ono-ha Itto Ryu that my friend Grigoris studies in Tokyo, the Tenjin Shin'yo Ryu of the Masters family, none of these have declined in my opinion. The people who train budo still train living budo.

"What has increased, is the number of people who do budo derived activities without a true martial core. There are plenty of people who study some form of budo as a hobby but without the spirit of life and death on a razor edge that fills budo with life. I've seen this in gendai arts and in koryu arts. Many people play judo without ever touching the spirit of budo. They only learn it as a sport, they only experience it as sport, and they only train in it as sport. They never do Kime No Kata with the feeling that uke is trying to kill them. They never get up after being thrown in randori thinking "I just died. If this were outside the dojo, I would be dead."

"I've seen koryu demonstrations where the koryu's spirit had died long ago. The students went through the motions of the kata, but with none of the lethal spirit necessary to give life to budo kata. They cut and thrust, strike and block, throw and pin, without any sense that what they are doing is training to deal with lethal intent. They have lost the spirit of their ryuha even as they maintain its form. Seeing groups like this do enbu always makes me sad. Often the shadow of the spirit of the ryuha can be glimpsed in the kata, but the people demonstrating it cannot grasp that spirit. Somewhere a teacher failed the ryuha by teaching the form without the spirit.

"Aikido gets a lot of bad press for not being truly martial, but that's the fault of the many teachers of Aikido who teach the art without the martial spirit that Ueshiba Morihei taught them with. When I read about many of the teachers who trained directly under the founder of aikido in the Aikido Sangenkai blog and other places, it's clear they learned budo. Especially for the pre-war deshi, training was done with the expectation that they would at some point be defending their art in a violent confrontation. Their training had that razor edge of life and death. They were there to learn real budo, and they treated their training that way. They got bumps and bruises and the occasional injury from pushing their training right out on the edge.

"I don't see that spirit often enough in today's aikido training. Too many people seem to think that going through the motions of kote gaeshi or irimi nage with a cooperative

► *Hiroshi Tada, Aikikai Aikido*

► *Gérard Blaize,*
Aikikai Aikido

partner is aikido training. It takes more than just going through the motions of a technique or a kata to bring training to life. Uke can't just be there for tori to do the kata or the technique on. That's one of my biggest problems with the way judo kata are trained these days. Too often uke is there to receive the technique and nothing more.

"For any budo to live, the role of uke must be an active one. It can't be passive. It is uke who brings training to life. This is something I find myself writing about again and again and again. Uke has to give tori enough resistance to make training a challenge, without giving so much resistance that they stop tori from doing anything. The amount of resistance is always relative to tori's skill at the specific thing being practiced. For an absolute beginner, just being there is enough resistance to make things difficult. Pretty soon though uke should be putting more effort into the initial attack and more resistance to the technique into the practice. Once a student has a fair level of experience the amount of speed and force in the attack, and the resistance to the technique, have to be fairly high. For a journeyman student, the attack should be completely real.

"By this I mean that if the attack is a strike to the head, tori should get thumped in the head if they don't get out of the way. If the attack is a grab, tori should find themselves being choked or thrown or pinned if they don't deal with the incoming power properly. At that level, techniques need to fail relatively often, with tori finding themselves countered when they don't get the technique right. I can't tell you how often I am doing a kata in Shinto Muso Ryu with a teacher and I find my jo swatted out of the way and a bokuto a centimeter from my eyes. This can go on for repetition after repetition until I get it right.

"It's not good for anyone to train a technique wrong.

"I think good budo can be an excellent resource for learning conflict management and resolution. In something like Shinto Muso Ryu or Kodokan Judo or Aikido there is much to learn about ways that conflict can be resolved. These aren't modern ideas though, and they assume that one side ends up in total control of the situation every time. There are no balanced outcomes in budo, not even in Kodokan Judo with its mandate of jita kyoei 自他共栄 or "mutual benefit and welfare" as it's often translated. People with little knowledge of Japanese translate aikido 合気道 as "way of harmony" and then impose very western ideas of what harmony means on it. The harmony of Japan, wa 和, has nothing to do with harmony that comes from a group of musicians working together and contributing equally to create beautiful music, or a dance troupe where everyone works together to create a spellbinding group performance. Wa is very top down in Japan. It is a NeoConfucian culture after all. The leaders, the shih in Chinese (which is by the way the shi in bushi 武士) are the senior sages of society and everyone is expected to conform to their example. When society naturally follows the example of the shih, there is harmony. At least that is the Confucian theory. Translating aiki 合気 as "harmony" leaves out the whole Confucian concept of what makes up social harmony every single time.

"Budo assumes one side is going to be in complete control at the end of the situation, and that side is imposing their will on the other side. This is true whether it is Katori Shinto Ryu slaying their opponent, Shinto Muso Ryu subduing their opponent without killing them, or even Aikido blending with an opponent and pinning them on the ground. These are varying degrees on a scale, but they all assume that one side completely dominates the other side. These are all great for winning at combat, but I'm not sure how useful they will be for improving relationships. I know I don't want to be in a relationship that is completely dominated by one side or the other.

"Where budo can teach useful lessons about relationships is in the way relationships are handled in the dojo. Ideally everyone in the dojo receives fundamental respect. Beginners

► *Howard Popkin and Peter Boylan*

► *The author with Matsuda Shigehar, Shinto Muso Ryu*

understand that they have nothing to contribute to class but their openness to learning and their willingness to accept corrections and work on developing their skills. They jump up to take care of things like sweeping and serving tea because these are the best ways they have of showing their appreciation for what they are receiving. Mid-rank students know more of what the dojo needs and have learned to take care of things required for running the dojo without being asked. They handle registrations and paperwork and all the minutiae that keeps a dojo running. Senior students support the head teacher and the dojocho with whatever is needed, including teaching classes. Sensei gets to worry about everything. Every role in the dojo is one of responsibility, not privilege. Changes in status are earned through effort, contribution and patience. Mature students work for the betterment of the dojo and all its members. Everyone works to understand their role in the dojo and puts forth their effort to contribute to the dojo as a whole. The rituals of the dojo, bowing, using titles like "sensei", politely changing training partners and approaching those you want to train with with humility all contribute to this.

"These are all things that can teach non-budo people a great deal about relationships. I don't think there is anything unique to budo in the above though. These can be found in ikebana, bonsai, kodo, cha no yu, and many other Japanese arts. They present a model for how mature people should treat each other and behave. These are useful models for relationships. I honestly don't see how the spirit of total domination and control that is central to budo training can offer much in the way of a model for relationships. Even a gentle ikkyo results with the uke face down on the floor submitting under the threat of having their arm broken. It may be my failing, but I can't see what this could teach anyone about maintaining good social relationships."

Gichin Funakoshi,
Shotokan Karate

About the Role of the Budo Teacher

"The role of the Budo teacher is one of the most complex and therefore most open to misunderstanding in the world of traditional Japanese classical arts. Where do you stand on the role of the Budo teacher? Should the relationship between teacher and student be based on moralistic elements as it is often interpreted, even unconsciously, in modern Budo? Are we to be the parents of our students?" [Simone Chierchini]

"In classical Japanese thought, the budo teacher is the shih 士, the sage leading training and setting the moral example for everyone in the dojo. Based on Confucius' teachings, the basic relationship model was always the parent-child relationship. I will admit that I'm not very excited about Confucian social theory, but I have to say that none of the westerners I have encountered making a big deal about rejecting the Confuican model had taken the time to really delve into it and understand the subtlety of Confucius' thought.

"For me, the dojo is one of the few places where the familial social model makes any sense. In many ways the sensei is the parent. In the dojo, sensei is responsible for the training and safety of everyone. That puts them in a role similar to a parent. Confucian thought is much more complex than just saying the parent-figure is responsible for the child-figure though. It's a complex of complementing responsibilities that the parent has to the child and the child has to the parent.

"The parent is both responsible for the child and responsible to the child. It is the parent's responsibilities to the child that are most often missed. The parent is responsible for the child's actions. This means that if the child does something seriously wrong, the parent is seen as being a poor parent. A good parent would not have created an atmosphere where the child would consider doing wrong. In Japan, the parent is responsible for cleaning up the messes of the child. In the budo world, the sensei is responsible for the actions of their deshi. If I do something wrong in the Japanese budo world, it always gets back to my teacher, regardless of whether it is small or large. I get kidded about the small mistakes and gently taught the correct way. I've seen what happens when someone does something majorly wrong. Sensei, and the whole dojo, are expected to make things right. Just the possibility of causing that sort of embarrassment to people I trust and respect is horrifying enough. Not to mention risking hamon.

"The students have a similar responsibility to their teacher. As one becomes senior in a dojo, one becomes more responsible for the decisions and actions taken by the dojo and by sensei. If sensei has too much to drink, it's the senior students' responsibility to make sure sensei doesn't do anything to embarrass himself or the dojo. If something does happen, the senior students' are responsible for discretely cleaning up the mess and for chastising sensei in the privacy of the dojo. Ideally, no one but senior students will see it, or even know about it.

"In Japan I've learned to embrace these sensei-deshi relationships. These relationships are not light burdens. As a non-Japanese, I worry about making some sort of faux pa whenever we go to budo events. I don't want to do anything

► *Morihei Ueshiba and Michio Hikitsuchi*

► Risuke Otake, Tenshin Shoden Katori Shinto Ryu

that would embarrass my dojo family. I also know that if I called one of my teachers in the middle of the night and asked for help, I'd get it.

"These sorts of relationships are only possible in small groups. Koryu dojos might have a dozen students. I've seen a few with two dozen. Even in those small groups, there are circles within circles. Those who have been students the longest are closest to sensei. There are those who have recently started and aren't really members of the dojo yet. In between are all degrees of closeness. A teacher can really get to know and develop this sort of relationship with a few students. In old Japan, where the dojo tended to be small groups, it was possible for the parent-student relationship to be the model for nearly all the relationships in the dojo. In big, gendai budo organizations this isn't possible. It's possible in some koryu groups because of their size and intimacy.

"I can't imagine a big dojo anywhere being able to support many of these relationships. Teachers are human with a limited amount of time and energy. The Confucian style parent-child relationship takes a lot of time and energy for each individual. It's even more unimaginable in a commercial relationship where the students have any degree of feeling they are paying for a product, even if the product is budo lessons.

"In the world of gendai budo I think we have to find a different model for our relationships than the traditional, Confucian, parent-child model. We need a model that can allow for students to study for years and then decide they want to do something else. We need one that can accommodate a looser type relationship more appropriate to the world we live in. My relationship with my gendai budo teachers is very different from that with my koryu budo teachers. With my koryu teachers there are maybe a dozen real students. There is time and energy to develop the sort of close bonds that Confucius valued. In the gendai budo dojos

I practice in, I am friends with the teachers I have known for many years. I respect their greater knowledge and skill. I like them as people. I don't seek the same sort of relationship with them and I'm sure they don't want that sort of relationship. The western teacher-student style relationship is much more appropriate for gendai budo dojos, in Japan and elsewhere."

► *Taizoh Nakagawa, master bladesmith*

RMG

Budo Training is Dangerous

"How do you judge the tendency that is manifesting in Gendai Budo to progressively eliminate certain techniques because they are considered potentially dangerous? Is it a sensible thing to adapt martial practice to the standards of our hyper-protective times? Or is risk inherent in the martial art, as in life, and without risk there is no experimentation and growth?" [Simone Chierchini]

"Budo training is dangerous. We hit each other, thow each other, lock up joints and strangle each other. I often hear the silly notion that Kano Jigoro took the dangerous techniques out of jujutsu to make Kodokan Judo. I don't know how anyone can practice even competitive judo and hold that opinion. Those are big, high amplitude throws. Even in the dojo on nice, forgiving tatami there are the occasional broken bones and other injuries. To be thrown with these techniques on any surface harder than tatami is to risk serious injury and death. Do a big harai goshi to someone and on the street and they are likely to have broken ribs, even if they know how to do good ukemi. If they don't, it's quite easy to make sure they smash their head into the concrete.

"All of the techniques in budo are potentially dangerous.

"What I have seen, and I generally support, is taking out techniques that are unnecessarily dangerous. Where techniques can be unnecessarily dangerous is in the dojo, during training. All the techniques in budo are dangerous when done correctly. The issue is techniques that are dangerous to even practice. The greatest example of this is the technique kani basami in judo. People noticed that ukes were having their legs dislocated and broken quite frequently, both in practice and in competition. There are videos circulating on the internet that show numerous examples of people having their legs destroyed with kani basami. Even in budo, you have to be able to practice the techniques in relative safety. If you are risking serious injury every time you go to the dojo, then the budo practice becomes a greater threat than any situation you are training to fight against.

"I'm not in favor of eliminating techniques because they are dangerous. If you take all the dangerous techniques out of judo or aikido you will be left with nothing but the etiquette. I am in favor of eliminating techniques that present an unnecessary risk of injury when you are learning and practicing them."

The Art of Peace?

"What do you think of those instructors who teach Aikido with The Art of Peace in their hands? Can one teach a martial art based on dubious westernized interpretations of geographically and culturally distant contexts, and personal moralistic overtones?" [Simone Chierchini]

"I find the idea of teaching Aikido with The Art Of Peace as any sort of guide to be extremely problematic. John Stevens is very earnest, but his translations I find are far from hitting the target. I'm waiting for Christopher Li to do a really definitive translation of Ueshiba Morihei's writings. I speak and read Japanese reasonably well, but not well enough to do justice to Ueshiba's poetry. He referenced classical Shinto stories and deities all over the place, and quoted both from classic works of Japanese literature that I've never been able to make myself sit down and read, much less get familiar enough with to be able to readly spot when they are quoted or referenced. Add the teachings of his beloved Omoto Kyo leader Deguchi Onisaburo on top of all that, and the mix requires a specialist with a deep understanding of the ideas that function as the foundation of his thought before they can be translated well. My Japanese skills help me notice when a translation has missed the mark, but there are very few with the sufficient background to even be sure where the target is.

"I think there are a lot of fluffy unicorns and rainbows floating around some Aikido dojos, and they do not contribute anything positive to the training or the culture. Ueshiba did preach about Aikido being the "art of peace" and "unifying the world." He was also a right-wing militarist from a Neo-Confucion culture. He would have had a great deal of difficulty wrapping his head around 21st century western ideas of what the art of peace means.

"I like the idea of bringing Eastern and Western ideas together. I think the synthesis is wonderful and can move both forward much further when taken together than either could manage on its own. However, you have to have a pretty solid foundation in the ideas of the other culture before you can bring them into your own effectively. Taosit ideas are a great example. I've been reading and rereading the Dao De Ching and Zhuang Zi for something like 40 years. I've read good translations and bad ones. Even the best translations cannot stand on their own. They must have a lot of background information to support them or you will quickly go off the rails of understanding into the realm of personal fantasy. You have to know something about the culture of China in the eras these were written, and the philosophical conversations that were happening to begin to unpack all of the ideas they contain.

"The same thing is true with Ueshiba's writings. I can't tell how many times I've seen "masakatsu agatsu" attributed to Ueshiba. It's not his. He was quoting the Kojiki, an 8th century collection of stories about the kami, the creation of Japan, and the relationship between the kami and men. Ueshiba liked the phrase a lot, and in Japan no one attributes it to him. Everyone knows where it comes from. The same is true for a lot of the things that are attributed to him outside Japan. He was a great martial artist, but I think we give him far too much credit for having unique teachings for society

► *Morihei Ueshiba pictured on the Mikasa warship*

and individuals. He borrowed extensively from classical Shinto, Shingon Buddhism, and Omoto Kyo teachings. If you're going to teach using Ueshiba's writings and you haven't taken the time to familiarize yourself with these, you won't be teaching anything Ueshiba thought or wrote. You'll be teaching the framework and ideas that you imposed on the translation. I mentioned the problem with translating wa 和 as harmony earlier, and those issues extend to many other terms that are quickly translated into other languages without the context that supports them in Japanese culture.

"Ueshiba's real legacy is his martial art. That's what he excelled at. Study that to learn his lessons. I cringe at the folks who soften aikido into a marshmallow because they've read one or two translations, or worse, none. There are plenty of people who read some of the ``biographies" of Ueshiba and think they understand what Ueshiba meant. I'm afraid the images of him as a peaceful, kind old man gently guiding us to a world of peace and harmony are about as far from the mark as is possible. He was a badass young man. He was a badass middle-aged man, and he continued to be a badass in his senior year. This is a guy who went with his guru to establish themselves in occupied China. He enthusiastically taught his martial art to the army and some of the worst militarists in Japan. I have never seen evidence that he disavowed or did anything to distance himself from all of this after the war.

"Ueshiba's martial art was always very martial. He acted from a place of strength, and he expected that from his students. I can't imagine how anyone could think that teaching Aikido as anything other than a martial art that makes one strong and able to impose your will on the world. Just because he taught that you should use very efficient techniques for doing that doesn't negate what he was teaching, but it can make it hard for people to grasp. The best Aikido that I've felt was both soft and devastating. I'm not exaggerating the "devastating" part. When I've been handled by great teachers, they completely control the situation and leave me with the options of doing things their way, or having to break my own arm to do anything else, and the throws have power in them. I hit the floor as hard as I do in judo. Aikido is about the application of power. That's its base."

Polarization

"Our society is going through a period of great polarization. There is no subject on which conflict does not develop in opposing ranks, even though the buzzwords of at least one of the factions in the field always seem to be 'respect, tolerance and inclusion'. How can Budo teachers, in their own small way, respond in action to what only sounds like empty words?" [Simone Chierchini]

"Polarization was a feature of the world that birthed classical bugei, with the wars in Japan leading up to the Tokugawa Era as well as the suspicions and divisions between the regions that supported the Tokugawa in the war and those that opposed them. During the 250 years of the Pax Tokugawa the bugei were taught and practiced in a world where most practitioners not only had the option of being armed all the time, but were expected to wear 2 swords as a symbol of their social rank. With all those weapons floating around, budo has always included healthy measures of respect and self-control.

"I think what budo has to offer is at the individual level. People who are confident in themselves and possess great quantities of self-control, have the strength to treat others with respect. To me, polarization is not the problem. People having very different opinions is normal. The problem is lack of respect and self-control.

"People who are not confident in themselves lack the inner resources to be truly respectful, and if they don't have plenty of self-control, they will be disrespectful to others. I think this is a place where budo has a lot to offer individuals. Good budo training builds individuals. Everyone focuses on techniques and physical skills, but more interesting for me is the mental skills and strength that budo, especially koryu budo, can develop.

"Everyone is familiar with budo instilling self-confidence for dealing with physical threats, but we don't often talk about what it does for people outside of physical self-defense. Good budo training stresses people both physically and mentally. It's the mental component that I think is the most important. If you don't have a solid mental foundation, your physical skills will be irrelevant. If you do have a strong mental foundation, you are less likely to be offended and angered by people with differing views and more likely to have the patience to hear people out, even those who are ranting like maniacs, without having your calm, heijoshin mind disturbed. Not being upset or allowing your mental balance to be undermined is the first step towards being able to respect, tolerate and include other people. Budo can do a lot at the individual level to foster strong, healthy minds that can deal with the stress of societies that seem to be pulling everyone to the extremes."

5/180

Budo Doesn't Require Rank

"What do grades and ranks have to do with Budo? I have never heard of a 5th dan fiddler or chef, nor a 7th dan boxer or soccer player... Their skills are linked to the publicly recognized value of what they do. Cristiano Ronaldo or Sokaku Takeda don't need any grades, why should we?" [Simone Chierchini]

"You'd be surprised at the practices that award dan ranks in Japan. I've seen them given out for karaoke! Japan is a very hierarchical, competitive society. Dan ranks are a great way to formalize everyone's place in the social structure in Japan. They allow everyone to see clearly where they and everyone else are in the club hierarchy and for people to get some recognition for what they are doing and accomplishing.

"What does all of this have to do with budo? Not a thing. I don't think Kano Jigoro Shihan created dan ranks in Kodokan Judo because he thought they would make people better judoka. I think he created them precisely because Japan is so hierarchical and everyone likes to know where they stand vis a vis everyone else. Kano Shihan created the first modern budo. His goal was to make Kodokan Judo a part of the education system and grow it into a single, national organization. This sort of thing had never been done with any budo system before. Cha No Yu had systems of certificates and licenses on a national level, but budo had been prevented from nationalizing by the Tokugawa shogunate. Kano Shihan was treading fresh ground and he had to be a little creative.

"Once he had a number of dojos practicing judo, and they were having competitions, a rank system probably seemed like a sensible way for people to explain their status in Kodokan Judo to people, especially strangers from different dojos. Large groups of strangers could train together and easily sort themselves by dan rank, and have a reasonable idea of each other's skill levels. I'm pretty sure using testing fees as a source of income was not one of the motivations. I also think it turned out to be a bad idea for budo.

"People hunting for rank became common and the dan system magnified the issues with hierarchy within Japanese society. I do both koryu and gendai budo. Koryu budo dojos are very much bands of brothers who train hard together and take care of each other. Rank isn't an issue, and folks work out the hierarchy issues pretty smoothly without rank. But koryu groups are small, even the big ones. Katori Shinto Ryu has fewer than 2000 students globally. Shinto Muso Ryu probably has far more, but they are not all in the same group. Each of us trains under a menkyo kaiden, and each menkyo kaiden is independent. The only students they have to worry about are their own, and no menkyo kaiden has very many. If any had more than 50 students they really claim as their own, I'd be shocked. You don't need many hierarchy markers in a group that small. Most of the folks doing Muso Jikiden Eishin Ryu and Muso Shinden Ryu are not training under a licensed teacher of the ryuha. They are training under someone who learned the kata set from someone who learned the kata set from a licensed teacher if they are lucky. My Muso Jikden Eishin Ryu teachers learned from licensed teachers, but they didn't receive licenses themselves. The only thing they had were dan ranks from the Kendo Federation. I

► *Haruna Matsuo,*
Muso Jikiden Eishin Ryu

► Takeda Sokaku,
Daito Ryu Aikijujutsu

had the privilege to know and do a little training with a licensed teacher of Muso Jikiden Eishin Ryu, but he wasn't my main teacher and I did not receive any scrolls or licenses from him. There are still a few licensed Muso Jikiden Eishin Ryu and Muso Shinden Ryu teachers out there, but you have to ask a lot of questions and search hard to find them.

Takeda Sokaku is a great example of how Japanese society loves hierarchy and precedence. I've never seen anything to convince me that he didn't create Daito Ryu himself. For whatever reason though, he felt he needed validation of his skill by saying that what he did was an old art and that he inherited it. This is a userful fig leaf in Japanese budo that allowed Takeda to teach a very new system while displaying humility about himself and his art. He didn't invent it, it was handed down to him. He's not responsible for making it a great system. Previous generations did that. I don't know if he really needed that fig leaf, or if he felt he needed it, or if he saw it as a good way to make a living charging students for what he taught. He grew up in the Bakumatsu and trained in Ono-ha Itto Ryu, so he knew how budo teachers made their living. There were regular training fees, and then there were extra fees every time you received a makimono or a license. It's how budo was taught in the Tokugawa Shogunate.

"Budo doesn't require any rank at all. It doesn't even require actual licenses. Look at all the people teaching and doing Muso Jikiden Eishin Ryu or Muso Shinden Ryu without ever getting a teaching license or even just a makimono of the system. Those people aren't members of the ryuha, but they are certainly practicing budo, and many of them are dedicated, excellent students. They will never receive rank or license or even membership in the living ryu, but they love what they are doing and do it without any expectation of rank or license. They are members of their local dojo, and have personal ties to their teacher. That's all they need. They train diligently. Thay have to be respected as budoka. They aren't looking for rank and don't need it.

"A different example would be all the people around the world training Hyoho Niten Ichi Ryu under Kajiya Takanori Soke or the folks training Shinkage Ryu under Yagyū Kōichi Taira Toshinobu Soke. Neither of these ryuha issue any sort of menkyo or makimono to anyone but the soke. Everyone else just trains. None of these people need rank and they clearly aren't interested in it if they train in an art that doesn't have any. For many, there is no need of any rank.

"Unfortunately, not all of us are well enough developed to be able to do without rank. I have a variety of ranks and licenses. For me they serve as indications of respect between myself and the people who gave them to me. When I was younger, I really liked the validation of my skill level represented by the changing colors of my belt as I progressed through the kyu ranks in judo. It focused me on the things necessary to achieve the next rank. Unfortunately I, like many, tended to ignore any part of judo that wasn't required for the next rank."

▸ *Yagyū Kōichi Taira Toshinobu, Shinkage Ryu*

"All You Have to Do Is Show up and Practice"

"In your 1999 thesis 'Aikido as Spiritual Practice in the United States' you made the following very interesting comments:

"(...) the only things that really count are that one comes to practice, and one puts forth sincere effort. This includes practising as much as one is able when injured (which the researcher did after spraining a wrist), and if one is unable to practise because of an injury, coming to practise to watch from the sidelines. This level of dedication is not in any way uncommon.

"This means of judging the community represents a radical departure from traditional American religion. It also makes it much more comfortable for people with, for example, radically different views on the founder and the creation of Aikido to practice together than American churches make it for people from very different religious views to worship together.

"This is the crux of the situation with the sacred narratives of Aikido. While they do exist, they are not overly important for the Aikido community. Even having any direct knowledge of them is not important. It is entirely possible for someone to achieve a high rank in Aikido without reading any of the Aikido literature cited here. In Aikido the only statement of faith that really counts is the statement made by your presence at practice on a regular basis." Could you expand on the above?" [Simone Chierchini]

"I'm impressed that you read my thesis. It's not particularly light reading.

"Japanese society is one in which actions are valued and words are not. It's what people see you do rather than what they hear you say that counts. No one really cares if you actively believe in the local kami. They care that you help out with the costs of caring for the local shrine and show up to help clean the grounds in the spring. They care that you show up at the local matsuri and give your support to the community that way. You're never asked to express your belief in the kami. Performance of the rituals is the strongest statement that is asked of people.

"The same is true for Japanese Buddhism. In Japan everyone's family belongs to a Buddhist temple. This is the result of laws during the Tokugawa Era requiring every family to be affiliated with a Buddhist temple for the practical purpose of keeping track of the population and getting everyone who had converted to give up Christianity. In addition, Shinto treats death as a form of contamination to be avoided, so there are no Shinto rites for the dead. When Buddhism arrived in Japan it brought with it an extensive set of rites for dealing with death. I would hazard a guess that most Japanese don't know which sect of Buddhism their family temple is a part of, but they do know which temple it is. That's because all of the family's ancestors are enshrined by the temple, and the temple priest performs regular rituals for the spirits of the ancestors. No one is ever asked if they believe in the Buddha or Amidha, or Jizo, or any of the other figures in Buddhism. You show up for the regular services for the ancestors and that's all that's expected. Your statement of belief or disbelief is irrelevant. It's what you do that they care about.

大阪
奥本

"This is in contrast with the religions that came out of the Middle East which are worried about your actions, but far more worried about your statements of belief and faith. Services rely on repetitions of statements of faith (the Lord's Prayer, the Nicene Creed, the Apostle's Creed, etc. in Christianity, the Shahada in Islam)

"Aikido is very Japanese. There are no creeds. There are no statements of faith. There is not even an expectation that you read any of the writings of the founder. All you have to do is show up and practice. That action is what is critical. I've trained with people who view Ueshiba Morihei as a kami of great power, and I've trained with people who view him as a powerful fighter whose skills they want to acquire. In the dojo community, both groups are considered aikidoka in good standing as long as they show up for training, put in effort and are respectful. It's easy to argue over statements of belief. It's a lot tougher to get into arguments over the truth of ikkyo. Ikkyo works. It's the affirmation of showing up for practice that counts.

"The arguments in the aikido community are more over who's technique is real. This is much more important than which dojo or organization you belong to. It's your actions, your technique that count. Whether you belong to the Aikikai or Yoshinkan or Tomiki or Ki Society or any of the other many aikido organizations is a distant second in how the community at large evaluates your commitment.

"If you look at the rank requirements, all of the aikido organizations have extensive technical requirements for promotion within the organization. I'm not aware of any that have requirements regarding what aikido literature you've read or if you believe that Ueshiba was a kami or had any sort of divine powers. It's all about showing up and putting in effort."

About Peter Boylan

Peter has been studying Japanese martial arts for over thirty years. He started with Kodokan Judo while in college and added iaido and jodo after moving to Japan, where he lived and studied for nearly seven years.

Currently, he is a fifth dan in All Japan Kendo Federation iaido, fifth dan in All Japan Kendo Federation jodo, third dan in Kodokan Judo, and holds a Shomokuroku in Shinto Muso Ryu and a Jun Shihan certificate in Shinto Hatakage Ryu.

When asked about his interests outside budo, the question seemed completely meaningless to him.

Photo Credits

Amdur, Ellis: 60
Assetai: 82
Bottoni, Paolo: 81
Boylan, Peter: 12, 95
Chierchini, Simone: 107, 120
Clausen, Kjarten: 39, 40
Corallini, Paolo N.: 53
Frye, Richard: 8, 11, 23, 27
Gordon, Charles: 15, 28, 31, 49
Gordon, Emily: 24, 39, 40
Ianett, Francesco: 46
Japan Press Illustrated Service: 36
Klens-Bigman, Deborah: 20, 50, 62
New York Budokai: 50
Public Domain: 32, 36, 44, 54, 58, 61-1, 61-2, 68, 71, 72, 88, 91, 92, 100, 103, 104, 115, 116, 119
ShinKenKai Iaido Dojo: 35
Takeda-Art: 43
Tsukahara, Hiroyuki: 19, 57, 62, 75

The Ran Network
https://therannetwork.com

The Aiki Dialogues

1. The Phenomenologist - Interview with Ellis Amdur
2. The Translator - Interview with Christopher Li
3. The Wrestler - Interview with Rionne "Fujiwara" McAvoy
4. The Traveler - "Find Your Way" - Interview with William T. Gillespie
5. Inryoku - "The Attractive Force" - Interview with Gérard Blaize
6. The Philosopher - Interview with André Cognard
7. The Hermeticist - Interview with Paolo N. Corallini
8. The Heir - Interview with Hiroo Mochizuki
9. The Parent - Interview with Simone Chierchini
10. The Sensei - About Yoji Fujimoto
11. The Teacher - Interview with Lia Suzuki
12. The Innovator - Interview with John Bailey
13. The Uchideshi - Interview with Jacques Payet
14. The Bodymind Educator - Interview with Paul Linden
15. The Budo Bum - Interview with Peter Boylan

Simone Chierchini: The Phenomenologist Interview with Ellis Amdur
The Aiki Dialogues - N. 1

Ellis Amdur is a renowned martial arts researcher, a teacher in two different surviving Koryū and a former Aikidō enthusiast.
His books on Aikidō and Budō are considered unique
in that he uses his own experiences, often hair-raising or outrageous, as illustrations of the principles about which he writes. His opinions are also backed by solid research and boots-on-the-ground experience. "The Phenomenologist" is no exception to that.

Simone Chierchini: The Translator - Interview with Christopher Li
The Aiki Dialogues - N. 2

Christopher Li is an instructor at the Aikido Sangenkai, a non-profit Aikidō group in Honolulu, Hawaii, on the island of Oahu. He has been training in traditional and modern Japanese martial arts since 1981, with more than twelve years of training while living in Japan. Chris calls himself a "hobbyist with a specialty", however, thanks to his research and writing he has made an important contribution to the understanding of modern Aikidō. His views on Aikidō, its history and future development are unconventional and often "politically incorrect" but he's not afraid to share them. This is not a book for those unwilling to discuss the official narrative of our art and its people.

Simone Chierchini: The Wrestler - Interview with Rionne McAvoy
The Aiki Dialogues - N. 3

From Taekwondo wonder kid to Karate State Champion, from Hiroshi Tada Sensei's Gessoji Dojo to the Aikikai Hombu Dojo and Yoshiaki Yokota sensei, Rionne "Fujiwara" McAvoy, a star in the toughest professional wrestling league in the world, Japan, has never been one for finding the easy way out. In "The Wrestler", Rionne McAvoy tells his story in martial arts and explains his strong views on Aikido, physical training and cross-training and reveals where he wants to go with his Aikido.

Simone Chierchini: The Traveler - Find Your Way Interview with William T. Gillespie
The Aiki Dialogues - N. 4

William T. Gillespie, the author of the book "Aikido in Japan and The Way Less Traveled", is a pioneer of Aikido in China. As the sign in his first Aikido Dojo in Los Angeles read, "Not even a million dollars can buy back one minute of your life". This is why W.T. Gillespie resigned from a professional career as a trial attorney in Los Angeles, to move to Tokyo to devote himself to intensively study Aikido at the Aikikai World Headquarters. Currently a 6th Dan Aikikai, his martial arts adventures in Japan and beyond to South East Asia, Korea and even The People's Republic of China became a fantastic journey of self-discovery and personal development that continues to unfold.

Simone Chierchini: Inryoku
The Attractive Force
Interview with Gérard Blaize
The Aiki Dialogues - N. 5

Gérard Blaize, the first non-Japanese Aikido expert to receive the rank of 7th dan Aikikai, spent five and a half years in Japan where he studied Aikido at the Hombu Dōjō in Tōkyō. In 1975, he met Michio Hikitsuchi, one of the most respected personal students of the founder of Aikido Morihei Ueshiba, and followed his sole guidance until his teacher's death in 2004. Hikitsuchi Sensei was a Shinto priest as well as a high ranked martial artist; in 1969 he was personally awarded the 10th Dan rank by O-sensei. Gérard Blaize has inherited and is still carrying the legacy of Hikitsuchi's holistic Aikido to this day.

Simone Chierchini: The Philosopher
Interview with André Cognard
The Aiki Dialogues - N. 6

André Cognard is one of the most authoritative voices in contemporary international Budo. Born in 1954 in France, he approached the world of martial arts at a very young age, dedicating himself to the intensive practice of various traditional Japanese disciplines. In 1973 he met Hirokazu Kobayashi sensei, a direct disciple of O-sensei Morihei Ueshiba.He received the rank of 8th Dan and on the death of his mentor inherited the leadership of the academy Kokusai Aikido Kenshukai Kobayashi Hirokazu Ryu. An "itinerant" teacher, a profound connoisseur of Japan and its traditions, André Cognard brings worldwide a technique – the Aikido of his Master; a human message – Aikido at the service of all; a spiritual message – Aikido which, like Man, reconnects with itself when it simply becomes Art.

Simone Chierchini: The Hermeticist
Interview with Paolo N. Corallini
The Aiki Dialogues - N. 7

Paolo N. Corallini has been practicing the Art of Aikido since 1969 and during his career he has held numerous positions in this art at national and international level. Author of many conferences on Aikido and its Spirituality, he has written 6 volumes on this martial art. A scholar of Eastern philosophies and religions such as Taoism, Shintoism, Esoteric Buddhism and Sufism, he loves the world of chivalric tradition in general and the Knights Templar in particular. In "The Hermeticist" Corallini sensei brings the reader from Iwama and his meeting with Morihiro Saito sensei to the complex interweaving between the different pedagogies in Aikido; from his memories of the man Morihiro Saito to the future of Aikido and much much more.

Adriano Amari: The Heir
Interview with Hiroo Mochizuki
The Aiki Dialogues - N. 8

Hiroo Mochizuki is the heir of a samurai family. Creator of Yoseikan Budo, he is a world-renowned expert in Japanese martial arts.
Son of the famous teacher Minoru Mochizuki, who is considered a Japanese national treasure and was also a direct student of Jigoro Kano and Morihei Ueshiba, the successor of a line of samurai, Hiroo Mochizuki was inspired by his forefathers combative spirit to create Yoseikan Budo.
He adapted the philosophy, pedagogy and traditional practice of martial arts to a new modern environment, as well as to contemporary combat techniques.
Besides practicing Mixed Martial Arts before people knew what MMA was, Hiroo Mochizuki has one of the most impressive records in the martial world.

Marco Rubatto: The Parent
Interview with Simone Chierchini
The Aiki Dialogues - N. 9

Simone Chierchini did not choose Budo, he "was there". For 50 years at the forefront and in an enviable position in the Aikido community, he had the opportunity to witness first-hand the major events that have accompanied the birth and development of Aikido in Italy and Europe. Simone began practicing Aikido at the age of eight and has travelled the world as a student and teacher of the art, changing friends, students and occupations but never forgetting to pack his sword, pen and camera. A direct pupil of Hideki Hosokawa and Yoji Fujimoto, Simone has recently founded Aikido Italia Network Publishing, the publishing house specialised in the dissemination of Aikidō and martial arts culture that hosts this interview.

Simone Chierchini: The Sensei
About Yoji Fujimoto
The Aiki Dialogues - N. 10

This publication endeavours to accomplish a very difficult task: that of bringing to life once again the voice and works of one of the most beloved figures of International Aikidō. Yoji Fujimoto sensei has been gone for nearly 10 years and has left behind thousands of students who have who have never stopped mourning him. Since 1971, the year of his arrival in Italy, Fujimoto sensei has dedicated his whole life and all his energy to the practice of Aikidō. In this book, some of Fujimoto sensei's senior students have tried, within the limits of their abilities and their memories, to evoke the figure and teaching of Fujimoto sensei.

Simone Chierchini: The Teacher
Interview with Lia Suzuki
The Aiki Dialogues - N. 11

Lia Suzuki, founder and director of Aikido Kenkyukai International USA, began her Aikido training in 1982 under William Gleason. She soon moved to Japan to train with Yoshinobu Takeda, one of Seigo Yamaguchi's most accomplished students. She lived in Japan and trained extensively in Aikido from 1987 to 1996. At the urging of Takeda shihan, Lia sensei returned to establish dojos in the USA in 1996. She currently holds the rank of 6th dan Aikikai and travels extensively as a guest instructor, conducting Aikido seminars in dojos around the world. Over the years, Lia sensei has dedicated her training to promoting inclusion in the world of Aikido and increasing the popularity of Aikido among young people.

Simone Chierchini: The Innovator
Interview with John Bailey
The Aiki Dialogues - N. 12

John Bailey studied Aikido under Tony Graziano and Tom Walker.
He is a graduate of Executive Security International and has an extensive background in security and investigations, having worked as a bouncer, security officer, bodyguard, undercover operative and tactical instructor. He's a life-long student of violence, the behavioural factors and practical implications of it.
He's presently focused on the navigation of crisis periods, and creating fulfilment through life design.
John has studied Aikido for four decades, the past two of which have been dedicated to exploring better ways to train and to teach the art in a quickly changing world.

Simone Chierchini:
The Bodymind Educator
Interview with Paul Linden
The Aiki Dialogues - N. 14

Founder of Being in Movement, Paul Linden, an Aikido teacher based in Columbus, Ohio, is a world leader in embodied training, having been active in the field for 40 years. Paul has been practising and teaching Aikido since 1969 and holds the rank of 6th dan. Author of numerous books and instructional videos on applications of body awareness training, Paul leads seminars around the world. Let's hear from him about his particular vision of what Aikido is and can offer to individuals and society in the future.

NEXT ISSUE:

The Aiki Dialogues N°16

S. Chierchini - R. Granati

The Iconoclast

Interview with
Luigi Carniel

Luigi Carniel's profound knowledge of classic bugei, his genuine desire to pass on unchanged the inheritance received from his notavle teachers, his vast martial expertise, stretching from Aikijujutsu to Katori Shinto Ryu, from Karate Wado Ryu to Gyokushin Ryu Jujutsu, and which also embraces the Japanese sword forging and polishing, is bound to fascinate. As Carniel Sensei often repeats, this age-old knowledge is comparable to a long chain that began centuries ago, a chain rooted in the very history of the samurai class. His task is to help form the next solid links that will allow this legacy to be passed on, unchanged, to subsequent generations.
The Iconoclast, a title that Luigi Carniel has earned for his characteristic of expressing what he thinks without mincing his words, is a text that informs and seduces.